James Martineau

Religion as affected by modern materialism: an address delivered in Manchester New college, London, at the opening of its eighty-ninth session, on Tuesday, October 6, 1874

James Martineau

Religion as affected by modern materialism: an address delivered in Manchester New college, London, at the opening of its eighty-ninth session, on Tuesday, October 6, 1874

ISBN/EAN: 9783337263966

Printed in Europe, USA, Canada, Australia, Japan

Cover: Foto ©Lupo / pixelio.de

More available books at **www.hansebooks.com**

RELIGION

AS AFFECTED BY

MODERN MATERIALISM:

An Address Delivered in Manchester New
College, London, at the Opening of
its Eighty-Ninth Session, on
Tuesday, October 6, 1874.

BY

JAMES MARTINEAU, LL.D.,

WITH AN INTRODUCTION BY THE

REV. HENRY W. BELLOWS, D. D.

NEW YORK:

G. P. PUTNAM'S SONS,

FOURTH AVENUE AND TWENTY-THIRD STREET,

1875.

PREFACE.

THE following Address, published by desire of my College, was much curtailed in oral delivery. As somewhat more patience may be hoped for in a reader than in a hearer, it now appears in full. The position assumed in it, of resistance to some speculative tendencies of modern physical research, is far from congenial to me: for it seems to place me in the wrong camp. But the exclusive pretension, long set up by Theology, to dominate the whole field of knowledge, seems now to have simply passed over to the material Sciences;—with the effect of inverting, rather than removing, a mischievous intellectual confusion, and shifting the darkness from outward Nature to Morals and Religion. I cannot admit that these are conquered provinces: and to re-affirm their independence, and protest against their absorption in a universal material empire, appears to me a pressing need alike for true philosophy and for the future of human character and society.

LONDON, Oct. 12, 1874.

INTRODUCTION.

Is the mind of man only the last product of the matter and force of our system of Nature, having its origin in the blind or purposeless chance which drifts into order and intelligence under a self-executing mandate or necessity, called the survival of the fittest? The alleged discovery and partial verification of the *method* by which Nature works, has aroused suspicions in many leading scientific minds that Nature is the only and the final reality; that we cannot get behind her phenomena—or rather, that there is nothing behind them; that matter and force are all we know or need to know, and that they have answered so many of our questions in regard to the origin of animal existence and instincts, and even human intelligence, that they need only to be persistently pressed in the same direction to tell us all we can ever know and all we ought to believe.

It is certain that a spirit older than matter, an intelligence other than human, a will freer than necessity, does not enter into the causes of things contemplated by the new science. It studies a mindless universe with the sharpened instincts of brutes who have slowly graduated into men—themselves the most intelligent essences in existence. Consciousness, reason, purpose, will, are results of blind, undesigning, unfeeling forces, inherent in matter. God is an unknown and unknowable Being, if He exists; but He is a needless hypothesis, and really only the reflection of man's own God-like thoughts and feelings. In its childhood humanity invented Him as the hiding-place of its own ignorance! It is against this hypothesis that Mr. Martineau directs his battery in the discourse which follows.

It is refreshing, in the midst of the crude replies which alarmed religionists are hastily hurling at the scientific assailants of faith in a

living God, to hear one thoroughly furnished
scholar, profound metaphysician, and earnest
Christian, entering his thoughtful and deeply-
considered protest against the tendencies or
conclusions of modern Materialism. Throughout the whole discussion of the last ten years,
between utilitarian philosophers and scientific
materialists, on one side, and believers in
intuitive morals and spiritual realities on the
other, Mr. Martineau has confessedly been the
leading champion of faith. No writer has ren-
dered, in this generation, such service to
Religion, assailed in its vital assumptions by
the arrogance of science, drunk with the new
wine of its recent victories. Happily unham-
pered with theological anachronisms or ecclesiastical entanglements ; free to acknowledge all
that science and experience can justly allege
against dogmatic inventions or out-lived traditions ; a frank confessor of whatever new
facts in the genesis of Nature modern science
has established ; tied to no creed and confess-
ing no intellectual accountableness to any
power less than the Eternal Reason—Mr.

Martineau, by his nature, culture, age, position, and character, is, of all living men, the best fitted to speak with the scientific mind of the day in the interests of religious faith, and more likely to be listened to by it with respect than any other voice. It is not as an enemy of science, much less as a friend of superstition; not as a disputer of the method of the Evolutionists, far less as a defender of bibliolatry or popular theology, that Mr. Martineau appears, but as one who hails and blesses all new truth derived from scientific sources, and especially in its influence in dispelling theological assumptions and time-hardened errors, himself a firm believer in spiritual realities and in a personal God.

It is instructive to find the disowned leaders in theological reform among the stoutest defenders of the essential postulates of religious faith, and to recognize in the foremost champions of spiritual realities against the assaults of modern Materialism, the knights who have swung the most ponderous battle-axes at the errors and exaggerations of what is called "orthodoxy." It must be a great puzzle to the English people to discover, in the stoutest, keenest, and most competent defender of essential Religion, openly assailed by the most gifted scientific minds, the person of a non-conformist Minister, representative of a body more neglected, disfellowshiped, and popularly associated with the enemies of faith, than any other in Christendom. It is a noble return to the church for the life-long suspicion and alienation it has visited upon one of its purest and most enlightened sons.

James Martineau needs no introduction to American thinkers, and I have not the presumption, in writing at the request of the American publishers this preface to his latest work, to hope to add anything to the attention this profound and brilliant paper will receive. I seek rather to avail myself of its attraction to win a little notice to suggestions that would find small audience out of such company.

RELIGION

AS AFFECTED BY

MODERN MATERIALISM.

THE College which places me here to-day
professes to select and qualify suitable men
for the Nonconformist Ministry; that is, the
headship of societies voluntarily formed for
the promotion of the Christian life. In carrying out its work, two rules have been
invariably observed: (1) the Special Studies
which deal with our sources of religious
faith—whether in the scrutiny of nature or
in the interpretation of sacred books—have
been left open to the play of all new lights of
thought and knowledge, and have promptly
reflected every well-grounded intellectual
change; and (2) the General Studies which
give the balanced aptitudes of a cultivated

mind have been made as extensive and thorough as the years at disposal would allow. In both these rules there is apparent a genuine thirst for a right apprehension of things, a contempt for the dangers of possible discovery, a persuasion that in the mind most large and luminous the springs of Religion have the freshest and the fullest flow ; together with the idea that the Preacher, instead of being the organ of a given theology, should himself, by the natural influence of mental superiority, pass to the front and take the lead in a regulated growth of opinion.

There have never been wanting prophets of ill who distrusted this method as rash. So much open air does not suit the closet divine ; such liability to change disappoints the fixed idea of the partisan ; and the " practical man " does not want his preacher's head made heavy with too much learning, or his faith attenuated in the vacuum of metaphysics. At the present moment these partial distrusts are superseded by a deeper and more comprehensive misgiving, affecting not the method

simply, but the aim and function of our
Institution. Side by side with the literary
pursuits of the scholar, the study of external
nature has always had a place of honor in our
traditions and our estimates of a manly edu-
cation ; and there is scarcely a special science
which has not some brilliant names that
range not far from the lines of our history ;
and from the favorite shelf of all our libraries,
the Principia of Newton, the Essays of
Franklin, the Papers of Priestley and Dalton,
the " Principles " of Lyell, the Biological
Treatises of Southwood Smith and Carpenter,
and the records of Botanical research by Sir
James Smith and the Hookers, look down
upon us with something of a personal interest.
The successive enlargements given by these
skilled interpreters to our earlier picture of
the world—the widening Space, the deepen-
ing vistas of Time, the new groups of chemical elements and the precision of their com-
binations, the detected marvels of physio-
logical structure, and the rapid filling-in of
missing links in the chain of organic life—

have been eagerly welcomed as adding a
glory to the realities around, and, by the
erection of fresh shrines and cloisters, turning
the simple temple in which we once stood
into a clustered magnificence. Thus it was,
so long as discoveries came upon us one by
one ; nor did any biblical chronology or
Apocalypse interfere with their proper evidence for an hour. But *now*—must we not
confess it ?—certain shadows of anxiety seem
to steal forth and mingle with the advancing
light of natural knowledge, and temper it to a
less genial warmth. It comes on, no longer
in the simple form of pulse after pulse of
positive and limited discovery, but with the
ambitious sweep of a universal theory, in
which facts given by observation, laws
gathered by induction, and conceptions furnished by the mind itself, are all wrought up
together as if of homogeneous validity. A
report is thus framed of the Genesis of things,
made up, indeed, of many true chapters of
Science, but systematized by the terms and
assumptions of a questionable, if not an un-

tenable, philosophy. To the inexpert reader this report seems to be all of one piece; and he is disturbed to find an account apparently complete of the " Whence and the Whither" of all things without recourse to aught that is divine; to see the refinements of organism and exactitudes of adaptation disenchanted of their wonder; to watch the beauty of the flower fade into a necessity; to learn that Man was never *intended* for his place upon this scene, and has no commission to fulfill, but is simply flung hither by the competitive passions of the most gifted brutes; and to be assured that the élite beings that tenant the earth tread each upon an infinite series of failures, and survive as trophies of immeasurable misery and death. Thus an apprehension has become widely spread, that Natural History and Science are destined to give the *coup de grâce* to all theology, and discharge the religious phenomena from human life; that churches and their symbols must disappear like the witches' chamber and the astrologists' tower; and that, as everything

above our nature is dark and void, those who
affect to lift it lead it nowhither, and must
take themselves away as "blind leaders of the
blind." Whether this apprehension is well
founded or not is a very grave question for
society in many relations; and is emphatically
urgent for those who educate men as spiritual
guides to others, and who can invest them
with no directing power except the native
force of a mind at one with the truth of
things and a heart of quickened sympathies.
Hitherto, they have been trained under the
assumptions that the Universe which includes
us and folds us round is the Life-dwelling of
an Eternal Mind ; that the World of our
abode is the scene of a Moral Government
incipient but not yet complete ; and that the
upper zones of Human Affection, above the
clouds of self and passion, take us into
the sphére of a Divine Communion. Into
this over-arching scene it is that growing
thought and enthusiasm have expanded to
catch their light and fire. And if " the new
faith " is to carry in it the contradictories of

these positions—if it leaves us to make what we can of a simply molecular universe, and a pessimist world, and an unappeasable battle of life—it will require another sort of Apostolate, and would make such a difference in the studies which it is reasonable to pursue, that it might be wisest for us to disband, and let the new Future preach its own gospel, and devise, if it can, the means of making the tidings "*glad.*" Better at once to own our occupation gone than to linger on sentimental sufferance, and accept the indulgent assurance that, though there is no longer any *truth* in religion, there is some nice feeling in it ; and that while, for all we have to teach, we might shut up to-morrow, we may harmlessly keep open still, as a nursery of "*Emotion.*"* I trust that, when "emotion" proves empty, we shall stamp it out, and get rid of it.

Though, however, no partnership between the physicist and the theologian can be formed on these terms of assigning the intellect to

---

* See Professor Tyndall's Address before the British Association ; with Additions, p. 61.

the one and the feelings to the other, may it not
be that, in the flurry of exultation and of
panic, they misconstrue their real position?
and that their relations, when calmly sur-
veyed, may not be in such a state of tension
as each is ready to believe? Looking on
their respective contentions from the external
position of logical observation, and without
presuming to call in question the received
inductions of the naturalist, I believe that
both parties mistake the bearing of those inductions upon Religion; and that, although
this bearing is in some aspects serious, it is
neither of the quality nor of the magnitude
frequently ascribed to it. I venture to affirm
that the essence of Religion, summed up in
the three assumptions already enumerated,
is independent of any possible results of the
natural sciences, and stands fast through the
various readings of the Genesis of things.

The unpracticed mind of simple times goes
out, it is true, upon everything *en masse*, and
indeterminately feels and thinks about itself
and the field of its existence, the inner and

the outer, the transient and the permanent,
the visible and the invisible : its knowledge
and its worship, the pictures of its fancy and
the intuition of its faith, are as yet a single
tissue, of which every broken thread rends and
deforms the whole. Hence the oldest sacred
traditions run into stories of world-building ;
and the earliest attempts at a systematic interpretation of nature, in which physical ideas
were clothed in mythical garb, are regarded
by Aristotle as "*theological.*" It must be ad-
mitted that our own age has not yet emerged
from this confusion. And in so far as Church
belief is still committed to a given cosmogony
and natural history of Man, it lies open to
scientific refutation, and has already received
from it many a wound under which it visibly
pines away. It is needless to say that the *new*
"book of Genesis," which resorts to Lucretius
for its "first beginnings," to protoplasm for its
fifth day, to "natural selection" for its Adam
and Eve, and to evolution for all the rest, con-
tradicts the *old* book at every point ; and inas-
.much as it dissipates the dream of Paradise,

and removes the tragedy of the Fall, cancels at
once the need and the scheme of Redemption,
and so leaves the historical churches of Europe
crumbling away from their very foundations.
If any one would know how utterly unpro-
ducible in modern daylight is the theology of
the symbolical books, how absolutely alien
from the real springs of our life, let him follow for a few hours the newest movement of
ecclesiastical reform, and listen to the reported
conferences at Bonn on the remedies for a
divided Christendom.   Scarcely could the
personal reappearance of Athanasius or Cyril
on the floor of the council-hall be more start-
ling, or the cries of anathema from the voices
of the ancient dead have a more wondrous
sound, than the reproduction, as hopes of the
future, by men of Munich, of Chester, of Pitts-
burg, and of the Eastern Church, of formulas
without meaning for the present, the eager
discussion of subtle varieties of falsehood, and
the anxious masking of their differences by
opaque phrases under which everybody man-
ages to look.   Such signs of strange intellectual

anachronism excuse the aversion with which
many a thoughtful man, with a heart still full
of reverence, turns away from all religious
association, and lives without a church. It
has been the infatuation of ecclesiastics to
miss the inner divine spirit that breathes
through the sources of their faith, and to
seize, as the materials of their system, the
perishable conceptions and unverified predic-
tions of more fervent but darker times; so
that, in the structure they have raised, all that
is most questionable in the legacy of the
past — obsolete Physics, mythical History,
Messianic Mythology, Apocalyptic prognosti-
cations—have been built into the very walls,
if not made the corner-stone, and now by their
inevitable decay threaten the whole with ruin.
Why, indeed, should I charge this infatuation
on councils and divines alone? It is not pro-
fessional, but human; it is a delusion which
affects us all. We are forever shaping our
representations of invisible things, in comparison with other men's notions, into forms
of definite opinion, and throwing them to the

front, as if they were the photographic equiv-
alent of our real faith.   Yet somehow the
essence of our religion never finds its way into
these frames of theory: as we put them together it slips away, and, if we turn to pursue
it, still retreats behind; ever ready to work
with the will, to unbind and sweeten the affections, and bathe the life with reverence; but
refusing to be seen, or to pass from a divine
hue of thinking into a human pattern of
thought.   The effects of this infatuation in
the founders of our civilization are disastrous
on both sides, not only to the Churches whose
system is undermined, but to the spirit of the
Science which undermines it.   It turns out
that, with the sun and moon and stars, and in
and on the earth both before and after the
appearance of our race, quite other things
have happened than those which the consecrated cosmogony recites: especially Man,
instead of falling from a higher state, has
risen from a lower, and inherits, instead of a
uniform corruption, a law of perpetual im-
provement; so that the real process has the

effect, not only of an enormous magnifier, but
of an inverting mirror, on the theological
picture. Yet, notwithstanding the deplorable
appearance to which that picture is thus reduced, it is exhibited afresh every week to
millions still taught to regard it as divine.
This is the mischief on the theologic side.
On the other hand, Science, in executing this
merited punishment, has borrowed from its
opponents one of their worst errors, in identi-
fying the anomalous or lawless with the divine,
and assuming that whatever falls within the
province of nature drops thereby out of relation to God. As the old story of Creation
called in the Supreme Power only by way of
supernatural paroxysm, to gain some fresh
start beyond the resources of the natural
order, so the new inquirers, on getting rid of
these crises, fancy that the Agent who had
been invoked for them is gone, and proclaim
at once that Matter without Thought is competent to all. In thus confounding the idea
of the Divine Mind with that of *miracle-worker*,
they do but go over to the theological camp,

and snatch thence its oldest and bluntest
weapon, which in modern conflict can only
burden the hand that wields it. How runs
the history of their alleged negative discovery?
The Naturalist was told in his youth that at
certain intervals—at the joints, for instance,
between successive species of organisms—acts
of sudden creation summoned fresh groups of
creatures out of nothing. These epochs he
attacks with riper knowledge ; he finds a series
of intermediary forms, and fragmentary lines
of suggestion for others ; and when the affinities are fairly complete, and the chasm in the
order of production is filled up, he turns upon
us, and says, "See, there is no break in the
chain of origination, however far back you
trace it ; we no more want a Divine Agent
there and *then*, than *here* and *now.*" Be it so ;
but it is precisely here and now that He is
needed, to be the fountain of orderly power,
and to render the tissue of laws intelligible
by his presence : his witness is found not only
in the gaps, but in the continuity of being—
not in the suspense, but in the everlasting flow

of change ; for the universe as known, being throughout a system of *Thought-relations*, can subsist only in an eternal Mind that thinks it.

In the whole history of the Genesis of things Religion must unconditionally surrender to the Sciences. Not indeed that it is without share in the great question of *Causality ;* but its concern with it is totally different from theirs ; for it asks only about the " *Whence*" of all phenomena, while they concentrate their scrutiny upon the " *How :* " by which I mean that their end is accomplished as soon as it has been found in what groups phenomena regularly cluster, and on what threads of succession they are strung, and into what classification their resemblances throw them. These are matters of fact, directly or circuitously ascertainable by perception, and remaining the same, *be their originating power what it may.* On *that* ulterior question the Sciences have nothing to say. And, on the other hand, when Religion here takes up her word and insists that the phenomena thus reduced to system are the product of *Mind*, she in no way prejudges the *modus operandi*, but is ready to accept whatever affinities of aspect, whatever adjustments of order, the skill of observers may reveal. On *these* investigations she has nothing to say. If indeed you could ever show that the method of the universe is one along which *no Mind could move*—that it is absolutely incoherent and unideal—you would destroy the possibility of Religion as a doctrine of Causality: only, however, by simultaneously discovering the impossibility of Science—which wholly consists in organizing the phenomena of the world into an intellectual scheme reflecting the structure of its archetype. That those who labor to render the universe *intelligible* should call in question its *relation to intelligence,* is one of those curious inconsistencies to which the ablest specialists are often the most liable when meditating in foreign fields. If it takes *Mind* to construe the world, how can the negation of Mind suffice to constitute it?

It is not in the history of Superstition alone that the human mind may be found struggling in the grasp of some mere nightmare of its own creation : a philosophical hypothesis may sit upon the breast with a weight not less oppressive and not more real; till a friendly touch or a dawning light breaks the spell, and reveals the quiet morning and the bed of rest. Is there, for instance, no logical illusion in the Materialist doctrine which in our time is proclaimed with so much pomp and resisted with so much passion ? "Matter is all I want," says the Physicist : "give me its atoms alone, and I will explain the universe." "Good; take as many of them as you please : see, they have all that is requisite to Body, being homogeneous extended solids." "That is not enough," he replies ; "it might do for Democritus and the mathematicians, but I must have somewhat more : the atoms must be not only in motion and of various shapes, but also of as many kinds as there may be chemical elements; for how could I ever get water, if I had only hydrogen molecules to work with?" "So be it," we shall say ; "only this is a considerable enlargement of your specified datum,

—in fact, a conversion of it into several; yet, even at the cost of its monism, your scheme seems hardly to gain its end; for by what manipulation of your resources will you, for example, educe *consciousness?* No organism can ever show you more than Matter moved; and, as Dubois-Reymond observes, there is an impassable chasm 'between definite movements of definite cerebral atoms and the primary facts which I can neither define nor deny—*I feel pain or pleasure, I taste a sweetness, smell a rose-scent, hear an organ tone, see red,* together with the no less immediate assurance they give, *therefore I exist:*' 'it remains,' he adds, 'entirely and forever inconceivable that it should signify a jot to a number of carbon and hydrogen and nitrogen and oxygen and other atoms how they lie and move;' 'in no way can one see how from their concurrence consciousness can arise.'*

---

* "Ueber die Grenzen des Naturerkennens," p. 29. Compare p. 20. "I will now prove, as I believe in a very cogent way, not only that, in the present state of our knowledge, Consciousness cannot be explained by

What say you to this problem?" "It does not daunt me at all," he declares : "of course you understand that my atoms have all along been affected by gravitation and polarity; and now I have only to insist, with Fechner,* on a difference among molecules; there are the *inorganic*, which can change only their *place*, like the particles in an undulation; and there are the *organic*, which can change their *order*, as in a globule that turns itself inside out. With an adequate number of these, our problem will be manageable." "Likely enough," we may say, " seeing how careful you are to provide for all emergencies ; and if any hitch should occur at the next step, where you will have to pass from mere sentiency to Thought and Will, you can again look in upon your atoms, and fling among them a handful of Leibnitz's monads, to serve as souls in little,

---

its material conditions,—which perhaps every one allows, —but that from the very nature of things it never will admit of explanation by these conditions."

* Einige Ideen zur Schöpfungs- und Entwickelungsgeschichte der Organismen, §§ i. ii.

and be ready, in a latent form, with that *Vor-stellungsfähigkeit* which our picturesque inter-preters of nature so much prize. But surely you must observe how this 'Matter' of yours alters its style with every change of service : starting as a beggar, with scarce a rag of 'property' to cover its bones, it turns up as a Prince, when large undertakings are wanted, loaded with investments, and within an inch of a plenipotentiary. In short, you give it precisely what you require to take from it ; and when your definition has made it ' preg-nant with all the future,' there is no wonder if from it all the future might be born."

"We must radically change our notions of Matter," says Professor Tyndall ; and then, he ventures to believe, it will answer all de-mands, carrying " the promise and potency of all terrestrial life."* If the measure of the required " change in our notions " had been

---

* Address before the British Association ; with Addi-tions, pp. 54, 55. Compare the statement, by Dubois-Reymond, of the opposite opinion, quoted supra, p. 28, note.

specified, the proposition would have had a real meaning, and been susceptible of a test. Without this precision, it only tells us, "Charge the word potentially with your quæsita, and I will promise to elicit them explicitly." It is easy traveling through the stages of such an hypothesis; you deposit at your bank a round sum ere you start; and, drawing on it piece-meal at every pause, complete your grand tour without a debt. Words, however, ere they can hold such richness of prerogative, will be found to have emerged from their physical meaning, and to be truly $\vartheta\epsilon o\varphi \acute{o}\rho\alpha$ $\acute{o}v\acute{o}\mu\alpha\tau\alpha$, —terms that bear God in them, and thus dissolve the very theory which they represent. Such extremely clever Matter—Matter that is up to everything, even to writing Hamlet, and finding out its own evolution, and substituting a molecular plébiscite for a divine monarchy of the world, may fairly be regarded as a little too modest in its disclaimer of the attributes of Mind.

Nor is the fallacy escaped by splitting our datum into two, and instead of crowding all

requisites into Matter, leaving it on its old
slender footing, and assuming along with it
Force as a distinct entity. The two postulates
will perform their promise, just like the one,
on condition that you secrete within them
in the germ all that you are to develop from
them as their fruit; and in this case the word
"*Force*" is the magical seed-vessel which is to
surprise us with the affluence of its contents.
The surprise is due to one or two nimble-
witted substitutions, of which a conjuror
might be proud, whereby unequals are shown
to be equals, and out of an acorn you hatch a
chicken. First, the noun *Force* is sent into
the plural (which of course is only itself in
another form), and so we get provided with
several of them. Next, as there is now a
class, the members must be distinguishable;
and, as they are all of them activities, they
will be known one from another by the sort
of work they do : one will be a mechanician—
another a chemist—a third will be a swift
runner along the tracks of life—a fourth will
find out all the rest—will do our reasoning

about them, and get up all our examinations
for us. The last of these, every one must own
—at least every one who has been graduated—
is much more dignified than the others ; and all
through we rise, at every step, from ruder to
more refined accomplishment. With things
thus settled, we seem to have found Plato's
ideal State, in which every order minds its
own business, and no element presumes to
cross the line and become something else.
Not so, however ; for, after thus differencing
the forces and keeping them under separate
covers, the next step is to unify them, and
show them all as the homogeneous contents
of a single receptacle. The forces, we are
assured, are interchangeable, and relieve each
other; when one has carried its message, it
hands the torch to another, and the light is
never quenched or the race arrested, but runs
an eternal round. But why then, you will
say, divide them first, only to unite them
afterwards ? Follow our logical wonder-
worker one move further, and you will see.
He has now, we may say, his four vessels

standing on the table; the contents of the whole are to be whisked into one; having them all, he has more ways than one of working out their equivalence; and it remains at his option, *which* he shall lift to let the mouse run out. For some reason, best known to himself, he never thinks of choosing the last; indeed it is pretty much to avoid this, and obtain other receptacles *empty of thought,* that he broke down the original unity. If he be a circumspect physiologist, he will probably prefer the third, and exhibit the universal principle as in some sense *living;* if he be a daring physicist, he will lay hold of the first, and pronounce *mechanical* dynamics good enough for the cosmos.

Am I asked to indicate the precise seat of fallacy in the hypothesis which I have ventured to criticise? The alleged division of forces, considered as something over and above the phenomena ascribed to them, is absolutely without ground; each of them, as apart from any other, has a purely ideal existence, without the slightest claim to objective reality.

Science, dividing its labors, has to break down phenomena into sets, according to their resemblances and the affinities of their conditions; it disposes them thus into natural provinces, the laws of which, when ascertained, give us the rules by which the phenomena assort themselves or successively arise—but nothing more. But whatever field we survey, we carry into it the belief, inherent in the constitution of the intellect itself, of a Causal Power as the source of every change : we believe it for each, we believe it for all : it repeats itself identically with every instance ; and when a multitude of instances are tied up together in virtue of their similarity and made into a class, this constantly recurring reference, this identity of relation to a power behind, is marked by giving that power a singular name ; as the phenomena of weight are labeled with the title *Gravitation*, expressing unity in their causal relation. Were we closeted with this group of facts alone, this unity would live in our minds without a rival, and we should have no numerical distinction in our account of force.

But, meanwhile, other observers have been
going through a like experience in some separate field; have gleaned and bound into a
sheaf its scattered mass of homogeneous
growths, and denoted them by another name
—say, *Electricity*—carrying in it the same
haunting reference to a source for them all.
Now, why is this a *new* name? Is it that we
have found a new *power?* Have we carried
our observation *behind the phenomena*, so as, in
either instance, to find any power at all?
Are the two cases differenced by anything else
than the dissimilarity of their phenomena?
Run over these distinctions, and, when you
have exhausted them, is there anything left by
which you can compare and set apart from
each other the respective producing forces?
All these questions must be answered in the
negative; the differentiations lie only in the
effects; the causal power is not *observed*, but
thought; and that thought is the same, not
only from instance to instance, but from field
to field; and by this sameness it cancels plu-
rality from Force, and reduces the story of

their transmigration into a scientific mythology. The distinctive names, therefore, mark
only differences in the *sets of phenomena;* they
are simply instruments of classification for
noticeable changes in nature, and carry no
partitions into the mysterious depths behind
the scenes. The dynamic catalogue being thus
left empty and cut down to a single term, do
we talk nonsense when we attach qualifying
epithets to the word *Force,* and speak of "*elec-
tric force,*" of "*nerve force,*" of "*polar force,*"
etc.? Not so; provided we mean by those
phrases simply, *Force, quantum sufficit,* now for
one set of phenomena, now for another, without
implication of other difference than that of the
seat and conditions and aspect of the manifes-
tations. But the moment we step across this
restriction, we are in the land of myths.

Power, then, is one and undivided. As external causality, it is not an *object of knowledge,*
but an *element given in the relations of knowledge, a condition of our thinking of phenomena
at all.* Were this all, our necessary belief in
it would be unattended by any *representation*

of it; it would remain an intellectual notion
(Begriff), and we could no more bring it before
the mind under any definite type than we can
the meaning of such words as "substance" and
"possibility." In one field, however, and no
more, it falls into coincidence with our experience; for we ourselves put forth power in the
exercise of Will and are personally conscious of
Causality; and this sample of *immediate*
knowledge because *self*-knowledge supplies us
with the means of *representing* to ourselves
what else we should have to *think* without a
type. Here, accordingly, we reach, I venture
to affirm, what we really mean, and what alone
saves us from the mere empty form of meaning, whenever we assent to the axiom of Causality. It is very true that the exercise of Will,
having more or less of complication, itself
admits of analysis; *intention* may play a larger
or smaller part, may leave less or more for the
share of automatic or impulsive activity; and
by letting the former withdraw into the back-
ground of our conception, we may come to
think of *causation apart from purpose*—which,

I suppose, is the *idea of Force.* But this is a
bare fiction of abstraction, shamming an inte-
gral reality ; an old soldier pensioned off from
actual duty, but allowed to wear his uniform
and look like what he was. Since we have to
assume causality for all things, and the only
causality we know is that of living mind, that
type has no legitimate competitor. Even if it
had, its sole adequacy would leave it in pos-
session of the field. For among the products
to be accounted for is the whole class and
hierarchy of *minds ;* and unless there is to be
more in the effect than in the cause, nothing
less than Mind is competent to realize a
scheme of being whose ranks ascend so high.
As for the plea—which has unhappily passed
into a common-place—that, even if it be so,
that transcendent object is beyond all cogni-
zance—I will only say that this doctrine of
Nescience stands in exactly the same relation
to causal power, whether you construe it as
Material Force or as Divine Agency. Neither
can be *observed ;* one or the other must be
assumed. If you admit to the category of

knowledge only what we learn by observation, particular or generalized, then is Force unknown ; if you extend the word to what is imported by the intellect itself into our cognitive acts, to make them such, then is God known.

This comment on current hypotheses refers to them only so far as they overstep the limits of Science, and aspire to the seat of judgment on ulterior questions of philosophy. So long as they simply descend upon this or that realm of nature, and try their strength there in simplifying its laws or rendering them deducible —or, passing from province to province, labor to formulate equations available for several or for all—they must be respectfully left to pursue their work; and whenever their authors present their demonstrated " system of the world," all reasonable men will learn it from them, whatever it may be, as scholars from a master. In the investigation of the genetic order of things, Theology is an intruder, and must stand aside. Religion first reaches its true ground, when, leaving the problem of what *has happened*, it takes its stand on what

forever is. * I do not say that it is indifferent
to us how antecedent ages have been filled,
and have brought up the march with which
we fall into step to-day; for we are beings of
large perspective, concentrating in us many
lines of distance and images that lie between

---

* This statement has been pronounced by a friendly
critic (*Spectator*, Oct. 17, p. 1293) "not only questionable,
but gravely misleading;" as implying "that if history
and science showed us constant degradation instead of
evolution of higher forms, and filled us with anticipa-
tions from which reasonable hope—hope, that is,
measured by experience—was utterly excluded, the
religion of the Soul would just as certainly assert the
supremacy of righteousness and the love of God, as she
does with the united voices of revelation and experience
to help her out."

If I had said that Religion has *no interest* in the history of nature and the world, this criticism would have
been just. But I cannot see how it applies to the positions which the text aims to make good, viz.: that Religion has no *locus standi* in investigations about the
order of phenomena in the past, but must make what it
can of that order as determined by scientific evidence:
and that Religion has a *locus standi*, where Science has
not, in the quest and cognition of the Cause that is behind all phenomena. To reach that Cause, there is no
need to go into the past, as though, being missed here,
He could be found there. But when once He has been
discerned through the proper organs of divine apprehension, the whole life of humanity is recognized as the

the eye and the horizon ; and what we see at
hand borrows a portion of its aspect from relation to remoter zones behind. But still, if
the light were all turned off from the Past,
and on facing it we looked only into the Night,
the reality for us is not *there*, but *here*, where
it is Day.   However the present may have
come about, I find myself in it: in whatever
way my faculties may have been determined,
faculties they are, and they give me insight
into my duty and outlook on my position :
however the world, of Nature and of Society,
may have grown to what it is, its scene con-
tains me, its relations twine around me, its
physiognomy appeals to me with a meaning
from behind itself.   If these data do not
suffice to show me my kinship with what is
above, below, around me, and find my moral
and spiritual place, I shall not be greatly

---

scene of His agency, and the past, no less than the present, has to be embraced in the religious interpretation of
the world, and becomes an object of sacred interest.
Though Religion, in taking its stand on what forever
is, *first reaches* its true ground, it does not follow that it
must always remain there.

·helped by discovering how many ages my constitution has been upon the stocks, and its antecedents been upon the way. The beings that touch me with their look and draw me out of myself, the duties that press upon my heart and hand, are on the spot, speaking to me while the clock ticks; and to love them aright, to serve them faithfully, and construct with them a true harmony of life, is the same task, whether I bear within me the inheritance of a million years, or, with all my surroundings, issued this morning from the dark.

Remaining then at home, and consulting the nature which we have and which we see, we find that, far from being self-inclosed, or related only to its visible dependencies, it turns a face, on more than one side, right towards the Infinite, and, often to the disregard of nearer things, moves hither or thither as if shrinking from a shadow advancing thence, or drawn by a light that wins it forward. We are constantly—even the most practical of us—seeing what is invisible and hearing what is inaudible, and permitting them

to send us on our way. Not left, like the mere
animal, to be the passive resultant of forces
without and instincts within, but invested with
an alternative power, we are conscious partners
in the architecture of our own character, and
know ourselves to be the bearers of a *trust ;*
and this fiduciary life takes us at once across
the boundary which separates nature from
what transcends it. Seducing appetites and
turbulent passions and ignoble ease never gain
our undivided ear ; while we bend to them,
there are pleading voices which distract us,
and which, if they do not save us, follow us
with an expostulating shame. Nor, if ever we
wake up and, kindle at the appeal of misery
and the cry of wrong, or with the spontaneous
fire of disinterested affection or devotion to
the true and good, can we construe them into
anything less than a Divine claim upon us :
we know their right over us at a glance ; we
feel on us their look of authority in reply ; if,
to our careless fancy, we were ever our own,
we can be so no more. Once stirred by the
higher springs of character, and possessed by

the yearning for the perfect mind, we are aware that to live out of these is our supreme obligation, and that for us nothing short of this is holy. To have *seen* the vision of the best and possible and *not* to pursue it, is to mar the true idea of our nature, and to fall from its heaven as a rebel and an outcast. This inner life of Conscience and ideal aspiration supplies the elements and sphere of Religion; and the discovery of Duty is as distinctly relative to an Objective Righteousness as the perception of Form to an external Space: it is a bondage, with superficial reluctance, but with deeper consent, to an invisible Highest; and both moral Fear and moral Love stand before the face of an authority which is the eternal reality of the holy, just, and true. On the first view, you might expect that the stronger the enthusiasm for goodness, and the surer the recoil from ill, so much the fitter would the mind be to stand alone· in its self-adequacy; yet it is precisely at such elevation that it most trusts in a Supreme Perfection to which it only faintly responds, and leans for support on that everlasting stay. The life of aspiration, attempting to nurse itself, soon pines and dies; it must breathe a diviner air, and take its thirst to unwasting springs; and wherever it settles into a quiet tension of the will, and an upturned look of the affections, it is sustained by habitual access to the Fountain of sanctity, and by the consciousness of an Infinite sympathy. Are not both the need and the existence of this objective sustaining power acknowledged by Mr. Matthew Arnold himself, when he insists on that strange entity, "That, not ourselves, *which makes for righteousness*"? By an abstraction, however, such a function cannot be discharged; nothing ever "makes for righteousness" but One who *is* righteous. To support and raise the less, there must be a greater; and that which does not think and will and love, whatever the drift of its blind power, may indeed be larger, but is not greater, than the sinning soul that longs for purity.

Now, so long as the devotee of Goodness is

possessed by a faith, not only in his own as-
pirations, but in an Infinite Mind which fos-
ters and secures them as counterparts of the
highest reality, it is of little moment ethically
what theory he adopts of their mode of origin
within him. Whether he takes them as intuitive data of his understanding, or, with
Hartley, as a transfiguration of sensible interests into a disinterested glory, or, with Dar-
win and Spencer, as the latest refinement of
animal instinct and discipline after percola-
ting · through uncounted generations,—that
which he has reached—be it first or last—is
at all events *the truth of things*, the primordial
and everlasting certainty, in comparison with
which all prior stages of training, if such there
were, give but dim gropings and transient
illusions. In Hartley himself, accordingly, a
doctrine essentially materialistic and carrying
in it the whole principle of Evolution, so far
as it could be epitomized in the individual's
life, easily blended with moral fervor and
even a mystic piety ; and, in Priestley, with a
noble heroism of veracity and an unswerving

confidence in the' perfect government of the
universe. But what if the process of atomic
development be taken as the *Substitute for
God*, not as His *method?* if you withdraw
from the beginning all *Idea* of what is to come
out at the end—all Model or Archetype to
control and direct the procedure, and restrain
the *possible* from running off indefinitely into
the false and wrong? Do you suppose that
the ethical results can be still the same? The
inevitable difference, I think, few considerate
persons will deny; and without attempt to
measure its amount, its chief feature may be
readily defined.

It was often said by both James and John
Stuart Mill, that you do not alter, much less
destroy, a feeling or sentiment by giving its
history: from whatever unexpected sources
its constituents may be gathered, when once
their confluence is complete the current they
form runs on the same, whether you know
them or not. How true this may be is exem-
plified by the younger Mill himself; who,
while resolving the moral sentiments into

simple pleasure and pain, and moral obligation into a balance of happiness, yet nobly protested that he would rather plunge into eternal anguish than falsely bend before an unrighteous power. If so it be, then one in whom benevolence, honor, purity, had reached their greatest refinement and most decisive clearness would suffer no change of moral consciousness, on becoming convinced that it is a "poetic thrill" of his "ganglia" * induced by the long breaking-in through which his progenitors have passed, in conformity with the system of organic modification that has deprived him of his fur and his tail. In spite of the apparent incongruity, let us grant that his higher affections will speak to him exactly as before, and make their claims felt by the same tones of sacred authority, so that they continue to subdue him in reverence or lift him as with inspiration. The surrender to them of heart and will under these conditions, the vow to abide by them and live in them,

---

* Professor Tyndall's Address, p. 49.

4

may still deserve acknowledgment as *Religion*
but, inasmuch as they have shrunk into mere
unaccredited subjective susceptibilities, they
have lost all support from Omniscient ap-
proval, and all presumable accordance with
the reality of things. For what *are* these
moral intensities of his nature, seen under his
new lights? Whence is their message? With
what right do they deliver it to him in that
imperative voice? and, if it be slighted, pros-
trate him with unspeakable compunction?
Are they an influx of Righteousness and Love
from the life of the universe? Do they report
the insight of beings more august and pure?
No; they are capitalized "experiences of util-
ity" and social coercion, the record of ances-
tral fears and satisfaction stored in his brain,
and reappearing with divine pretensions, only
because their animal origin is forgotten; or,
under another aspect, they are the newest
advantage won by gregarious creatures in "the
struggle for existence." From such an origin
it is impossible to extract credentials for any
elevated claim; so that although low begin-

nings may lead, in the natural order, to what
is better than themselves—as a Julia may be
the mother of an Agrippina—yet in such case
the superiority lies in new endowment, which
is *not* contained in the inheritance. For such
new endowment as we gain in the ascent from
interest to conscience the theory of trans-
mission cannot provide. If the coarse and tur-
bid springs of barbarous life, filtered through
innumerable organisms, flow limpid and spark-
ling at last, the element is still the same,
though the sediment is left behind; and as it
would need a diviner power to turn the water
into wine, so Prudence, run however fine, social
Conformity, however swift and spontaneous,
can never convert themselves into Obligation.
Hence arises, I think, an inevitable contradiction between the scientific hypothesis and
the personal characteristics of a high-souled
disciple of the modern negative doctrine. For
his supreme affections no adequate object
and no corresponding source is offered in the
universe; if they look back for their cradle,
they see through the forest the cabin of the

savage or the lair of the brute; if they look forth for their justifying reality and end, they fling vain arms aloft and embrace a vacancy. They cannot defend, yet cannot relinquish, their own enthusiasm : they bear him forward upon heroic lines that sweep wide of his own theory; and, transcending their own reputed origin and environment, they float upon vapors and are empty, self-poised by their own heat. One or two instances will illustrate the way in which what is best in our humanity is left, in the current doctrine, unsupported by the real constitution of the world.

Compassion—the instinctive response to the spectacle of misery—has a twofold express- iveness : it is in us a protesting vote against the sufferings we see, and a sign of faith that they are not ultimate, but remediable. Its singularity is, to be not one of these alone, but both. Were it a simple repugnance, it would drive us from its object; but it is an *aversion which attracts:* it snatches us with a bound to the very thing we hate, and not with hostile rush, but with softened tread and gentle words and uplifting hand. And what is the secret of this transfiguration of horror into love ? It could never be but for the implicit assurance that for these wounds there is healing possible, if the nursing care does not delay. Should we not say then, if we trusted its own word about itself, that this principle, so deep and intense in our unfolded nature, is an evident provision for a world of *hopeful sorrow?* It is distinctly relative to pain, and would be out of place in a scene laid out for happiness alone ; yet treats that pain as transient, and on passing into the cloud already sees the opening through. It enters the infirmary of human ills with the tender and cheerful trust of the young Sister of mercy, who binds herself to the perpetual presence of human maladies, that she may be forever giving them their discharge. Compassion institutes a strange order of servitude : it sets the strong to obey the weak, the man and woman to wait upon the child, and youth and beauty to kneel and bend before decrepitude and deformity. How then do the drift and

faith of this instinct agree with the method of
the outer world as now interpreted? Do they
copy it exactly, and find encouragement from
the great example? On the contrary, Nature,
it is customary to say, is *pitiless*, and, while
ever moving on, makes no step but by crush-
ing a thousand-fold more sentient life than
she ultimately sets up, and sets up none that
does not devour what is already there. The
battle of existence rages through all time and
in every field; and its rule is to give no
quarter—to dispatch the maimed, to overtake
the halt, to trip up the blind, and drive the
fugitive host over the precipice into the sea.
Nature is fond of the mighty, and kicks
the feeble; and, while forever multiplying
wretchedness, has no patience with it when it
looks up and moans. And so all-pervading is
this rule, that evil, we are told, cannot really
be put down, but only masked and diverted;
if you suppress it here, it will break out there;
the fire of anguish still rolls below and has
alternate vents; when you stop up Ætna, it
will blot out Sodom and Gomorrah, and bury

the cities of the plain. Who can deny that such teachings as these set the outer universe and our inner nature at its best at hopeless variance with one another? Do they not depress the moral power to which we owe the most humanizing features of our civilization? We have not to go far for a practical answer. Within a few weeks the question has been raised whether the recent flow of commiseration towards the famine-stricken districts of India does not offend against the Law of Nature for reducing a superfluous population; and whether there were not advantages in the old method of taking no notice of these things, and letting Death pass freely over his threshing-floor and bury the human chaff quietly out of the way. Moral enthusiasm makes many a mischievous mistake in its haste and blindness, and greatly needs the guidance of wiser thought; but this tone of moral skepticism, which disparages the very springs of generous labor, and treats them as follies laughed at by the cynicism of Nature, is a thousand-fold more desolating. For it

carries poison to the very roots of good. It
is as the bursting-out of salt-springs in the
valley of fruits ; it soaks through the prolific
soil of all the virtues, and turns the promise of
Eden into a Dead Sea shore.

Beyond the range of the merely com-
passionate impulse, *Self-forgetfulness* in love
for others has a foremost place in our
ideal of character, and our deep homage
as representing the true end of our humanity. We exact it from ourselves, and the
poor answer we make to the demand costs us
many a sigh ; and till we can break the bonds
that hold us to our own center, and lose our
self-care in constant sacrifice, a shadow of
silent reproach lies upon our heart. Who is
so faultless, or so obtuse, as to be ignorant
what shame there is, not only in snatched advantages and ease retained to others' loss, but
in ungentle words, in wronging judgment
within our private thoughts alone ; nay, in
simple blindness to what is passing in another's mind? Who does not upbraid himself for his slowness in those sympathies which

are as a multiplying mirror to the joys of life,
reflecting them in endless play? And the
grace so imperfect in ourselves wins our in-
stant veneration when realized in others. The
historical admirations of men are often, indeed, drawn to a very different type of character: for Genius and Will have their magnificence as well as Goodness its beauty: but
before the eye of a purified reverence, neither
the giants of force nor the recluses of saintly
austerity stand on so high a pedestal as the
devoted benefactors of mankind. The heroes
of honor are great; but the heroes of service
are greater; nor does any appeal speak more
home to us than a true story of life risked, of
ambitions dropped, of repose surrendered, of
temper molded, of all things serenely en-
dured—perhaps unnoticed and in exile—at
some call of sweet or high affection. Is then
this religion of Self-sacrifice the counterpart
of the behavior of the objective world? Is
the same principle to be found dominating on
that great scale? Far from it. *There*, we
are informed, the only rule is *self-assertion:*

the all-determining Law is relentless competition for superior advantage ; the condition of obeying which is, that you are to forego nothing, and never to miss an opportunity of pushing a rival over, and seizing the prey before he is on his feet again. We look without, and see the irresistible fact of selfish scramble : we look within, and find the irresistible faith of unselfish abnegation. So here, again, Morals are unnatural, and Nature is unmoral : and if, beyond Nature, there is nothing supreme in both relations to determine the subordination and resolve the contradiction, he who would be loyal to the higher call must be so without ground of trust ; if he will not betray his secret ideal, he must follow it unverified, as a mystic enchantment of his own mind.

Once more : the *Sense of Duty* enforces the suggestions of these and other affections by an authority which we recognize as at once within us and over us, and making them more than *impulses*, more than *ideals*, and establishing them in *binding* relations with our Will.

The rudest self-knowledge must own that the consciousness of *Moral Obligation* is an experience *sui generis*, separated by deep distinctions from *outward necessity* on the one hand, and *inward desire* upon the other ; and the only psychology which can bridge over these distinctions is that which escapes with its analysis into prehistoric ages, and finds it easy to grow vision out of touch, and read back all differentiation into sameness. No one would carry off the problem into that darkness who could deal with it in the present daylight : so, we may take it as confessed, that *to us* the suasion of Right speaks with a voice which no charming of pleasure and no chorus of opinion can ever learn to mimic. To disregard *them* is a simple matter of courage ; we defy them, and are free : but if from *it* we turn away, we hear pursuing feet behind : and should we stop our ears, we feel upon us the grasp of an awful hand. Moral good would, in our apprehension, cease to be what it is, were it constituted by any natural good, or related to it otherwise than as its superior. It is not a *personal* end—one among the many satisfactions assigned to the separate activities of our constitution : else, it would be at our disposal, and we might forego it. Others are our partners in it : for it sets up *Rights* as counterparts to *Duties*, and widens by its reciprocity into a common element of Humanity. Is *that* then its native home? Have men created it, as an expression of their general wish—a concentrated code of civic police? We cannot rest in this : for no aggregate of wills, no public meeting of mankind, though it got together all generations and all contemporary tribes, could by vote make perfidy a virtue and turn pity into a crime. Moral Right is thus no *local* essence; but by its centrifugal force, relatively to our abode, slips off the earth and assumes an absolute universality as the law of all free agency. That it should present itself to us in this transcendent aspect is intelligible enough, if it be identified with the Universal Mind, and thence imparted to dependent natures permitted to be like Him : for, in that case,

the related feelings and convictions are *true ;*
in the order of reality, Righteousness *is* prior
to the pains and pleasures of our particular
faculties and the natural exigencies of our
collective life ; and our allegiance is due to an
eternal Perfection which penetrates the moral
structure of all worlds. How, then, does this
intuitive faith of our responsible will, this
worship of an eternally Holy, stand with the
cosmical conceptions now tyrannizing over
the imaginations of men ? It encounters the
shock of contemptuous contradiction. Ethically, we are assured, the known world cul-
minates in us. Before us, there was nothing
morally good : over us, there is nothing morally better : Man himself is here the supreme
being in the universe. In the just, the benefi-
cent, the true, there is no pre-existence : they
are not the roots of reality, but the last
blossoms of the human phenomena. And
even there, the fair show which gives them
their repute of an ethereal beauty is but the
play of an ideal light upon coarse materials ;—
rude pleasures and ruder constraints are all

that remain when the increments of fancy
have fallen away. The real world provides
interests alone ; which, when adequately
masked, call themselves virtues and pass
for something new : and, duped by this illusion, we dream of a realm of authoritative
Duty, in which the earth is but a province of
a supramundane moral empire. And so, we
must conclude, the conscience which lives on
this sublime but empty vision has transcended
the tuition of Nature, and, in growing wiser
than its teacher, has lost its foothold on
reality, only to lean on a phantom of Divine
support.

On the hypothesis of a Mindless universe,
such is the fatal breach between the highest
inward life of man and his picture of the outer
world. All that is subjectively noblest turns
out to be the objectively hollowest ; and the
ideal, whether in life and character, or in the
beauty of the earth and heaven, which he had
taken to be the secret meaning of the Real,
is repudiated by it, and floats through space
as a homeless outcast. Even in this its

desolation a devoted disciple will say, " I will follow thee whithersoever thou goest;" but how heavy the cross which he will have to bear! Religion, under such conditions, is a defiance of inexorable material laws in favor of a better which they have created but cannot sustain—a reaction of man against Nature, which he has transcended—a withdrawal of the Self which a resistless force pushes to the front—a preservation of the weak whom Necessity crushes, a sympathy with sufferings which life relentlessly sets up—a recognition of authoritative Duty which cannot be. Or will you perhaps insist that, in this contrariety between thought and fact, Religion must take the other side, discharge the $\vartheta\varepsilon\tilde{\iota}\alpha$ $o\nu\varepsilon\acute{\iota}\rho\alpha\tau\alpha$ as illusory, and in her homage hold fast to the solid world? This might perhaps in some sense be, if you only gave us a world which it was possible to respect. But, by a curious though intelligible affinity, the modern doctrine allies itself with an unflinching pessimism; it plays the cynic to the universe—penetrates behind its grand and gracious airs, and detects its manifold blunders and impostures : what skill it has it cannot help ; and the only faults and horrors that are *not* in it are those which are too bad to live.   Human life, which is the summit that has been won, is pronounced but a poor affair at best; and the scene which spreads below and around is but as a battle-field at night-fall, with a few victors taking their faint shout away, and leaving the plain crowded with wounds and vocal with agony.   Existence itself, insists Hartmann, is an evil, in proportion as its range is larger and you know it more, and that of cultivated men is worst of all ; * and the constitution of the world (so stupidly does it work) would be an unpardonable crime, did it issue from a power that knew what it was about. †   How can these malcontents find any *Religion* in obeying such a power?   Can they approach it with contumely at one moment, and with devotion at the next?   If they think so ill of Nature, there can be no *reverence* in their ser-

---

* Philosophie des Unbewussten, c. xii., p. 598.

† Ap. Strauss : der alte und der neue Glaube, p. 223.

vice of her laws : on the contrary, they aban-
don what they revere, to bend before what
they revile. To this humiliation the more
magnanimous spirits will never stoop; they
will find some excuse for still clinging to the
ideal forms they cannot verify ; will go apart
with them with a high-toned love which stops
short of faith, but is full of faithfulness ; will
linger near the springs of poetry and art, and
there forget awhile the disenchanted Actual ;
and will wonder, perhaps, whether this half-
consecrated ground may not suffice, when the
temples are gone, to give an asylum to the
worshipers. Such loyalty of heart towards
the harmonies that *ought* to prevail, with dis-
affection towards the discords that *do* prevail,
may indeed lift the character of a man to an
elevation half divine ; and in his presence,
Nature, were she not blind, might start to see
that she had produced a god. But, for all
that, she is not going to succumb to him ; she
can call up her lower brood to suppress him,
or monsters to chain him to her rock. He
contends with the lower forces, believing them

5

to be the stronger, and fights his losing battle against hordes of inferiors ever swarming to overwhelm what is too good for the world. Such religion as remains to him is a religion of despair—a pathetic defiance of an eternal baser power. And if there be anything tragic in earth or heaven, it is the proud desolation of a mind which has to regard itself as highest, to know itself the seat of some love and justice and devotion to the good, and to look upon the system of the universe as cruel, ugly, stupid, and mean. The most touching episodes of history are perhaps those which disclose the life of genius and virtue under some capricious and ignoble tyranny—asserting itself in the ostracism of an Aristides, the hemlock-cup of Socrates, the blood-bath of Thrasea; and no other than this is the life of every man who, walking only by his purest inner lights, finds that they illumine no nature but his own, and are baffled and quenched by the outer darkness.

It cannot be denied that there does exist this contrariety between the modern materialistic philosophy and religious faith. It cannot be believed that this contrariety is chargeable on any mutual contradiction among the human faculties themselves. Were we really placed between two informants that said "*Yes*" at the right ear, and "*No*" at the left, we should simply be without cognitive endowment at all, and all the pulsations of thought would cancel each other and die. Can we end the strife by separating the provinces of the two opposites, and saying that the function of the one is *to know*, of the other *to create?* * Certainly "creative" power is something grand, and Theology should perhaps feel honored to be invested with it. But, alas! a *known* materialism and a *created* God presents a combination which thought repudiates and reverence abhors; and the suggestion of which must be met with the counter-affirmations, that the atomic hypothesis is a thing *not known, but created;* while God is *not created, but*

---

* Professor Tyndall's Address, p. 64.

known. The only possible basis for a treaty of alliance between the tendencies now in conflict is not in lodging the one in the Reason, and the other in the Imagination, in order to keep them from quarreling, but in recognizing a duality in the functions of Reason itself, according as it deals with phenomena or their ground, with law or with causality, with material consecution or with moral alternatives, with the definite relations of space and time and motion, or with the indefinite intensities of beauty and values of affection which bear us to the infinitely Good. When once this adjustment of functions has been considerately made, the disturbed equilibrium of minds will be reinstated, the panic and the arrogance of our time will disappear, and the progress of the intellect will no longer shake the soul from her everlasting rest.

www.ingramcontent.com/pod-product-compliance
Lightning Source LLC
Chambersburg PA
CBHW030716110426
42739CB00030B/596